Using Theatrical Stage Magic to Assess Cognitive Development

Exploring Fundamental Building Blocks in Childhood Development with Conjuring, Comedy and Sleight of Hand

by Rick Saldan

DEDICATION

This book is dedicated to the tireless souls with endless love, passion and patience who continually give of themselves to raise our children of the next generation. May you find numerous sources for strength, recreation and encouragement to recharge your batteries in powerful ways.

CONTENTS

For My Next Trick: Creating the Show

In working to set up this assessment and evaluation,

I found myself in a most difficult position of trying

to explain to my wife's family of this psychological

assessment that I wanted to conduct with their

children.

I could sense by the questions they were asking my

wife, that they were growing more and more

concerned as the conversation wore on. What kind

of results was I looking for? Would there be any

physical or emotional discomfort involved? Would

the children be upset in any manner? Are there any costs involved? My youngest niece, Bella, was age 4. Her older sister, Gabriella, was age 6.

It seemed to be getting more and more ridiculous, and I could see my wife growing tired of playing the role of middle man in trying to sell the idea to her brother on the telephone. Suddenly, the perfect answer seemed to present itself on the spur of the moment.

Like a delicious steak suddenly appearing to the stranded tourist lost in a sea of desert sand, the perfect solution to our spiraling conundrum instantly flashed before my eyes. I asked my wife to hand me the telephone, and I blurted out that we are offering to come over to their home and conduct a small magic show for their children. Just like real magic, these ten words suddenly transformed the energy of the conversation quite noticeably.

My brother-in-law audibly laughed and exclaimed, "Oh! I see!" and I could tell that he was instantly hooked and we would be closing the sale within another minute or two. His response also betrayed the fact that he felt his sister didn't quite understand what I was offering, and I must confess my guilt for allowing him to believe this was indeed the case, so that I might camouflage the fact that I had just thought of the idea only a mere few seconds before snatching the telephone away.

Sure enough, my brother-in-law readily agreed. I continued the thinly veiled subterfuge by further stating that it would be an educational format and that I was looking to try out some new ideas for teaching children some concepts with this program, such as sharing is caring and other helpful concepts along those lines.

Once again, the visual cortex loaned me yet another helping hand, and the brain flashed on the screen a video clip of me teaching the children how to perform a magic trick, so that I might prod here and there in hopes of uncovering some deep psychological nuggets of truth. Indeed, the subterfuge seemed to be taking on a life of its own, as I found that my own excitement level was intensifying as I was growing in admiration of the sheer cleverness of implementing the covert cover of using a magic show as a diversionary tool for conducting psychological research among O.P.C. (hereinafter a reference for "Other People's Children").

Responding to the very helpful suggestion raised by the visual cortex of my brain, I suddenly blurted out, "Oh, and I'll be teaching the children a few simple magic tricks, as well."

Sure enough, my Kreskin-like ability for sensing that this deal would be closed within a few minutes had truly come to pass. (I quickly thought to myself, now if I only I could enhance my Kreskin abilities by duplicating his world famous stage illusion of being able to find a paycheck that might be hidden anywhere among the audience members.)

This was getting better and better by the minute, because my wife's ever cautious and somewhat overly protective in-laws were now very excited that Mr. Magic would be coming over to the house to entertain the children, but now I found that I also was growing in enthusiasm for the undertaking as I now had the challenging mission of reviewing and hunting for those things which might correspond with some magic trick that I had collecting dust among the countless magic effects scattered all throughout my ever shrinking domicile.

I smiled to myself, as comical visions danced through my mind of psychologists all over the world one day employing a similar subterfuge of magical mayhem serving to disguise a psychological intrusion and exploration into the minds of both adult and child audience members, without any of them ever knowing that their inner processes had been probed and duly mapped without ever a wary parent raising a single solitary suspect concern. That is surely one of the great features and benefits of possessing the skill set of being a modern day conjuror and prestidigitator.

Without further ado, we now press on to the background and logistical details of the newly spawned "Operation Magic". Our target audience would be a dyad of two young toddlers. Bella, age 4, and her older sister, Gabriella, age 6. Both parents are employed at Cooper Hospital.

Donald is a respiratory therapist, and his wife Debbie is a nurse. Based on the past observations of their spending habits, their automobiles, and their very large gorgeous contemporary home, I might guess their combined income to be in the range of $120,000 to $150,000 per year.

Both children do go to public school, but they live in a high income neighborhood, and their public schools possess an excellent reputation for being fine schools.

Their home life and parental authority figures are what we might refer to as a typical conservative Asian parenting style, where such families place a relatively higher level of importance upon respect, discipline and diligence on the part of the youth themselves.

Unlike many American families, there is absolutely no sound of a blaring television coming from any of the rooms found around the household. Bella and Gabriella's parents believe in the age old idiom of "garbage in, garbage out", and they therefore dutifully monitor any influences that might be seeping into the minds of their children.

____

CHAPTER TWO

Pick A Card, Any Card:
Physical Development

After performing several of my standard opening magic effects, I felt that I had successfully connected with my two young nieces and that they were fully involved with the magic show.

I had magically produced my beautiful white cockatoo parrot, Gabriella (no connection with the name of my young niece, Gabriella), as well as two doves and a bunny. Their full attention was zeroed in on me, and they were hanging on each and every word that I spoke. As an experienced entertainer, I have found that I can sense and even gauge this

relative level of connectedness with audiences while

I am performing up on the stage. I have also felt this

same capability when out on a speaking

engagement, and not performing a magic show for

entertainment.

The ability to accurately gauge my level of rapport

with any audience has been repeatedly confirmed

by the after-event evaluations that are given out to

audience members by the client company.

This reminds me of Piaget's "intuitive thought

substage", where young children somehow know

something, but yet they did not arrive at that

knowledge by following a series of rational thinking or deliberate analysis (Gonzalez-DeHass, 29).

With everything in place, and my nieces plugged into the show, I was ready to switch gears and put on my researcher hat. To conduct my experiment for this section on physical development, I chose to explore their ability for learning a new task.

To put to the test the ability for my young magical mentorees to employ their hand-eye coordination, I decided I would walk them through the steps of how to make a small coin apparently disappear from their own little hands. This is a simple task for those children with more developed hand-eye coordination who might be a little older than my two nieces, as the areas of the brain related to such functions undergoes myelination and this serves to greatly impact the speed and efficiency making succinct hand-eye tasks become more fluid by age 4 in early childhood development (Anand, 15).

I recall thinking about this while considering what effects I would try to teach my protégés, and my immediate hypothesis was that Bella, age 4, would most likely become a bit flustered in trying to learn the sleight of hand skills in making a small coin disappear.

I predicted likewise that her older sister, Gabriella, age 6, would be more adept at picking up this new skill. My original hypothesis proved incorrect, as both girls were able to master the skill much more quickly than quite a number of adults that I have taught this basic trick to in my past shows.

To my surprise, both Bella and Gabriella immediately internalized the eight step process for making the coin disappear. I could not readily account for the reason why they both learned the effect so quickly as compared to hundreds of other people that I took the trick to.

I know that their parents encourage them both to learn to play the piano, and suspect that this might have accelerated their natural abilities of eye-hand coordination. It is important to note that I have taught this effect to an estimated 4,000+ people, and have been able to categorize the types of people who will learn the effect quickly, as opposed to those who will struggle and require more time and coaching to learn the effect.

As my benchmark, I look back to the countless wonderful experiences I had while serving as the house magician at the Split Rock Resort for nearly two years (October, 2007 – July, 2009). These were some of the most amazing and delightful audiences I have ever had. Always a lively, energetic and fun loving audience, I performed my weekly Friday evening show which was then followed by my "Magician's Apprentice Contest", whereby I employed the same format of the famous television show, "America's Got Talent" and children and adults would first learn a magic trick, and then perform that same trick in front of a panel of judges of their peers. Over the course of that nearly two years time in teaching the effect to an estimated 4,000 children and adults, it gave me some insight as to how quickly the average person might be able to learn this simple sleight of hand coin trick.

Over time, I noticed that younger children in the age range of 8 – 10 years of age were much more adept at learning this sleight of hand coin trick than were those children who were older. Additionally, I observed over time that more than 90% of adults who attempted to learn the eight step process for making a coin disappear had great difficulty.

For those adults who were determined to learn it, it always took them at least three times longer to learn the coin trick than the younger children in the age range of 8 – 10 years old. This large gap seems to be supported by C.L. Grady's 2008 research where he contrasts younger adults and older adults, and reports that older adults exhibit increased brain activity in the parietal and frontal brain regions while they are performing tasks that require them to focus and be attentive. (Bremner, 172).

Additionally, I saw that boys were able to master the effect faster than were girls. My personal observation of gender differences in eye-hand coordination appears to be supported by the fact that specialized portions of the parietal lobe that

function in such visuospatial skills is actually
physical larger in males than it is in females. (Ray,
97). While the text does not specifically state eye-
hand coordination, I do suspect that this is indeed
the case.

As a quick sidebar issue, I was motivated by
intellectual curiosity, and wanted to know if
researchers had ever been able to determine what
part of the brain actually contains the
'programming' for conducting such eye-hand
coordination so as to be able to proficiently conduct
the day to day tasks which might range from
picking up a book, to tying shoe laces, catching a
ball or driving a car.

We know that the ability for the brain to conduct such eye-hand coordination is begins very early in the life of a human being and this is recognized as Piaget's fourth sensorimotor substage, which develops in young infants between 8 and 12 months of age. (Martin, 40).

When researchers want to learn which part of the brain is performing a task, there are several tools that they might employ in mapping out a specific brain process. One such diagnostic neuroimaging tool is the use of positron emission tomography, which can detect changes in blood flow in the brain (Farah, 37).

I found it interesting that researchers from Emory and the University of California, Los Angeles, were able to pinpoint the area of the brain which is responsible for such eye-hand coordination. In order to achieve this goal for pinpointing the location, Garrett E. Alexander, professor of neurology at the School of Medicine, had experimenters wear glasses which contained prisms, and the brains of the subjects then were forced to recalibrate the function of eye-hand coordination in order to perform their normal day to day tasks with these glasses that contained prisms over the eye piece section. By employing positron emission tomography that detected the change in blood flow in the brain, researchers where able to successfully pinpoint this function as to be occurring within a

small section of the posterior parietal cortex.

CHAPTER THREE

Abracadabra: Cognitive Development

Next I resumed the magic show portion of my theatrical undertaking, and performed an effect where it appears that I am pulling silver dollars from thin air. I would show the girls that my hands are empty, then stretch and reach up into the empty air space around me, and a large silver dollar would magically appear at my fingertips.

I would toss the coin into a shiny metal bucket, specifically chosen because the reverberation is quite loud as the coin clanks against the sides of the metal bucket. This effect employs a few comedy routines as well, which gets the children laughing as silver dollars are magically produced from their ears, their hair, their sneakers, and so forth.

After gauging that they were fully reconnected and plugged in once again, I was ready to switch back to the ever so subtle researcher mode and conduct my next experiment. By this time, Donald, their father, had heard the commotion and squeals of delight and had quietly wandered into the living room to observe the show.

Not wanting to tip my hand, I fortunately had a piece of magic apparatus that would enable me to further conceal my true mission of psychological

investigation. Once again, spur of the moment

thinking had sparked yet another fruitful stream of

creativity that I would not have otherwise enjoyed if

things went differently. I'll explain shortly.

Next up at bat was the "beaker test" for

conservation abilities on the part of my two lovely

nieces. (Shaffer, 60). I had several sized glass tubes,

as well as a "magician's pitcher" of fake milk.

I chose two glass tumblers of equal size, and poured

equal amounts of milk into these tumblers. I pointed

out to the children and their father that each tumbler

had the same amount of milk. Next, I showed them

a new cylinder, which was much thinner in diameter,

and very tall. I poured the fake milk from one

tumbler into that one. I showed a fourth glass cup,

which was very large in diameter, but only one

fourth the size of the tall cylinder.

I poured the second tumbler of fake milk into that

one. I asked my three audience members which had

more milk, the tall and thin cylinder, or the short

and thicker glass cup. I assumed that the might

have different answers, so I asked them first not to

answer out loud until I pointed to each of them one

at a time.

My hypothesis was that definitely the older niece

would realize that I still was using the same amount,

but I was not sure how the younger niece Bella

would react. She could go either way. After witnessing the speed at which she learned the vanishing coin trick, I assumed that she would perceive the fact that I was using the same amount of milk in each circumstance.

To my surprise, both girls answered incorrectly. (Yes, fortunately their father readily understood it was the same amount!). According to Piaget, not passing this conservation test indicates that the girls are at the preoperational stage of cognitive development. (Shaffer, 57). Given their apparent intelligence in so many other areas, I was genuinely surprised (and somewhat disappointed) that both girls failed what would seem a very obvious transference, and felt that surely the six year old niece would have discerned the true facts of the matter.

In response to this surprising twist, a few possibilities present themselves. Since I asked the four year old niece Bella first, it is possible that Gabriella just went along with Bella's response kind of as a group cohesion factor.

Secondly, there is a small chance that Gabriella was shielding her sister from embarrassment by giving the same answer, even though she realized it was not an accurate answer. I have seen Gabriella act in a protective manner in the past shielding her younger sister, and consider this to be a possibility, albeit somewhat remote. A third option might have been that she was getting a little tired, and perhaps such fatigue might have been distracting her from the facts of the case at hand. Finally, the fourth option is that perhaps Gabriella really did believe that they were indeed now two different amount of the fake milk.

After all, this was in the context of a magic show, and perhaps she believed that I had performed a magic trick and had changed the amount of milk. Unfortunately, I was not presenting my little experiments in true controlled laboratory circumstances, so it was not possible in this format to isolate the underlying cause.

Earlier I had alluded to having a trick up my sleeve that was there at my fingertips quite by accident. Now this is rather funny. I had been using what is called a "magician's milk pitcher".

This is an apparatus that is gimmicked in a way that performs a magic trick. This next step was not pre-planned, but it presented itself as a surprise ending and the idea popped into my mind when their father had wandered in to observe.

Now I would snag him, as well. Just for his benefit, I then took the tall thin cylinder, and poured the fake milk into the milk pitcher. Next I pulled out a fifth container. This was a small jar, slightly larger than a baby food jar. I took the pitcher of milk, and poured almost the full contents of the milk into that tiny little baby food jar. Clearly, what I had just done was absolutely impossible.

With a slight smirk on my face, I raised the jar and the other tumbler to the father and asked which had more milk in it. He had been set up! He laughed with amazement at the impossible thing he had just witnessed with this own eyes!

I will break the magician's golden rule and explain what was done so that you can appreciate the finesse of this which, again, happened only by chance and last minute thinking. The gimmicked milk pitcher has a hidden compartment built into it. The magician can appear to be pouring out most of the milk, but, in reality, approximately 80% of the milk is now going into a hidden container. To the untrained observer, it looked like I had just poured half a quart of milk into a small jar.

Clearly impossible! It certainly made for a wonderful surprise ending that I will have to remember for the next time I want to do something similar.

Hocus Pocus:
Socio-Emotional Development

From the magician's standpoint, this phase of my

clandestine research mission that was thinly veiled

as a private magic show for two (plus Dad!) was

probably the most challenging to conjure up a

magical effect that tied in with one of the concepts

in this section of the text.

Much of this topic relates --to child abuse, and that

did not really seem an appropriate topic to dive into

without some negative backlash in one format or

another.

Still struggling with a logical tie-in, I chose to bring

along my head chopper illusion and see what kind

of response I might be able to elicit that might

present itself as valid research for this undertaking.

The head chopper illusion that I own is a beautiful

stage illusion that has a worth exceeding four

thousand dollars.

Most stage illusions are in that price range, but this

piece is particularly special due to its powerful

visual illusion. Unlike all other head choppers and

guillotines, this model is transparent.

Its inner workings are completely hidden from the

audience, and the transparent casing leads the

audience to more fully believe that the big metal

blade really is going into the neck of the victim, er,

ah, I mean the volunteer.

I asked Donald if he would please assist me in our

next magic effect. Situated off to the side of the

living room was the head chopper, which was

hidden from view and covered with a cloth blanket.

I wheeled this over to where Donald was standing.

With a smile to the two daughters, I quickly

whisked the blanket off of the apparatus to expose

glistening silver metal and wood head chopper. As

hoped, the girls both said "wow" in unison! This

illusion can look quite formidable, that is for certain.

Off to the side I had a cardboard box that contained a head of lettuce, and several carrots. I asked Donald to hand me these and they were placed into the holder of the head chopper.

The shiny metal blade was inserted, and forcefully pushed down as it sheared cleanly through the head of lettuce and the carrots. All of the severed vegetables dramatically flew into the air.

I asked Donald if he would please be willing to place his own head where the severed head of lettuce was dramatically parted in two only seconds ago. He laughed nervously, and shook his head with a big "no!"

Next I asked the girls, "Let me ask you, why is it that your daddy does not want to put his head right there where the lettuce was?"

They said he did not want to have his head chopped off. I asked, "Do you think he is afraid? Is he a scaredy cat?" The older daughter Gabriella said, "I would be afraid.

I don't want someone to chop my head off." The younger daughter Bella started to look a little nervous, so I realized I couldn't play this up too much. I asked Gabriella, "How do you feel when your daddy might be doing something that is dangerous?" She said, "I don't want my dad to ever get hurt." Gabriella was illustrating what Eisenberg,

Fabes & Spinrad refer to as "empathy", because she was able to zero in on how her father was feeling after witness sing the metal blade swiftly slicing through the head of lettuce. (Gilman, 120).

Sensing an opportunity to go a little further, I asked Gabriella, "But what if I could use some magic? What if I could say some magic words and your daddy's head would not be hurt?"

Admittedly, I was fishing for an answer. Gabriella looked at her father, and then looked at me. It looked as if she was about to say something, but then she did not. I did not see true fear in her eyes, or else I would have stopped. Instead, it seemed more like she felt she had to be respectful and say the right thing that would honor her father, or something along those lines. Not quite knowing what would be okay for her to respond, she instead became reluctant to say anything further. I could see that her eyes were lit up with emotion, but it seemed more like anticipation mixed with amusement of sorts.

Feeling a lull, I told the still reluctant father, "Donald, I will promise you that if you give me your trust, nothing will happen to you. What do you say, are you willing to step up and give it a try?" He was again smiling and laughing and shaking his head no. This can be an uncomfortable spot with a stage performer, because you don't want to bring up a volunteer that you have to send back to their seating. It looks bad for your volunteer, and it looks foolish for the magician. A bit awkward for all parties involved.

Wanting to move things forward, I said, "Donald, I'll tell you what – if you give this a try, I will teach you that trick where you can turn one dollar into a hundred dollar bill. How about it, are you willing to give it a try?"

He smiled and reluctantly agreed. With great drama and theater, Donald placed his head into the opening of the head chopper, and I magically placed the shiny metal blade right through his neck and completely out the other side. Fortunately I had brought my bucket along, just in case the magic did not work, because I didn't want Donald to lose his head over this!

For the closing effect for the evening, I asked the girls if they had ever had any dreams where they were able to fly through the skies. Both said no. I asked if they had ever dreamed of having wings like a bird, and being able to fly away into the clear blue skies. Both said no. Time to try another approach. I said, "Girls, wouldn't it be amazing, if one of you were able to float up off the ground. Do one of you want to give it a try?"

It seemed before I even finished asking the question, the five year old Bella had jumped up and was ready to try the levitation effect. This reminded me of the many times I had seen that the oldest child in a family has a tendency to be a little more timid and fearful than the younger siblings. I can recall seeing such a situation quite a number of times over the years.

The oldest child often seems to be one that struggles with shyness, or anxiety, or is not willing to try new things. While the younger siblings— and most often it is generally the youngest of all of the children— are more often than not the child that seems completely fearless and free of any anxieties about trying something new. I've seen this with a variety of circumstances, such as the oldest child being afraid of roller coasters, but the youngest child very eager to try something new and exciting.

I do not have a concrete answer for that dynamic that I have seen repeatedly, but our text indirectly suggests a few possibilities that might be tied with birth order.

We see that the firstborn child frequently experiences lavish love and attention until the second child comes along. Since an infant requires such extensive amounts of care and attention, that firstborn might be feeling a sense of bewildered abandonment with all energies being devoted to the newly born infant. (Carducci, 157). Personally, I am of the opinion that once that seed of anxiety and self doubt is planted into the heart and mind of the first born at such young tender ages (i.e., age five and under), that individual will wrestle with such feelings for the remainder of their lives. Sometimes such individuals will go to great extremes in hopes of over compensating and ridding themselves of such nagging feelings of inadequacy or anxiety, but they find that they are never completely 100% free of such feelings no matter what they do, or what great conquests they are able to engineer in their lives.

With my little niece Bella now up front and ready for the levitation illusion, I spread out a blanket on top of a board and asked her to lay down on it.

I took part of the blank and covered her slightly. With her sister and father looking on, I slowly removed the board that she was laying on, and, yes, our darling little Bella floated there in mid-air. Both

onlookers were smiling with delight, and her father

jumped up to go grab his digital camera.

Nothing Up My Sleeve: Suggestions to Caregivers

One concern that I had today, and in other visits to Donald's house in the past, is the underlying feeling that his protection and sheltering of Bella and Gabriella might be a bit too extensive. Sometimes if children are sheltered too much, there are negative repercussions that frequently are at risk of coming forth later on in life.

For example, some children who grow up in a strongly sheltered environment find that they are ill-equipped to cope in a world that they might find too aggressive. They did not endure the battles of peer group conflicts, and did not develop the social skills that are critical to successfully interacting with the bullies and manipulators of this world.

As a result, they can fall into traps and become easy prey when such people are encountered out in the working world. Such personalities will always make themselves known no matter what job or career you undertake. If not from a coworker, then often manipulation and bullying can come from a boss or supervisor.

The impact can be powerfully detrimental and shatter an otherwise promising career. What would be somewhat effortless for a "regular" person to circumnavigate can then be a living nightmare for the individual who has absolutely no exposure and experience in effectively managing the bullies of this world who seek to take advantage of you.

CHAPTER SIX

Now Where Did That Rabbit Run Off To? Something Special

I always thoroughly enjoy myself when I go to visit my brother-in-law and his family. They are such genuine people that truly radiate warmth and caring. My wife and her siblings all grew up in the Philippines. Their culture always impresses me, as nearly every single Filipino person I have ever met all seem to be well balanced, laid back, easy going and nurturing towards everyone else.

From a parental standpoint, I see that Donald is a very unique and probably somewhat rare parent (especially these days!) that is loving, nurturing, supportive and fair minded. I have the opinion that he views his role of father and husband as his number one job in this world. (Unlike many American fathers who view their family role as secondary to their career, or other interests).

His dedication as a loving father and good husband is exceptionally evident each and every time that I go visit with him and his family. I can see in the eyes of his children and wife that they all love Donald and respect him deeply.

He is a very good father to his two daughters. They know that his love is genuine and beyond measure. He does not spoil them in any manner, but he provides a high quality of living for them all with a beautiful home and a good income. Yet, I do not detect any haughtiness in him or his family members. They do not look down on others who might be less fortunate.

Sadly, many children across America do not experience such love and acceptance in their families. For most, they spend the rest of their lives wrestling with feelings of inadequacy. Such children grow up feeling unworthy of love. They fault themselves. This carries on through the years up into their own marriage and the workplace.

(McBride, 7).

CHAPTER SEVEN

Presto:
The Real Magic

As a child I grew up watching the hit television series, "The Brady Bunch". I believed that the Brady family was the supreme all time role model to be admired and emulated by American families across the country. However, after coming to know my brother-in-law fairly well these past several years, I would have to say that I now view his family in that light, and view Donald as a father that would be best emulated as a role model.

Donald has one of the most beautiful homes I have ever seen (from the inside!), and yet he is a kind and compassionate individual that always opens his home up to others. He always gives to charities and tithes his income to the local church. He is a warm and embraceable man that everyone looks up to.

I admire the skill that Donald has in rearing his child. All children, no matter who they are, will have their bad days when temper tantrums flare up and jealousies kick in. Donald seems to always instinctively know how to handle such situations in the most effective manner.

As a father, he has the very special gift of being strong yet humble simultaneously. Most people would think that these two traits are mutually exclusive of one another, but Donald is the first father that I have met that can somehow display both character traits simultaneously. There are no pompous or false airs about him, despite him having achieved great successes in his lifetime. The love he has for other human beings are genuine and heart felt. He is truly a good man, and a genuine gentleman. These are the types of character traits that I would like to adopt and manifest in my own life.

WORKS CITED

Anand, KV. *Infant and Child Psychology*. Raleigh, NC: Lulu, 2010. Print.

Bremner, J. Gavin. *An Introduction to Developmental Psychology*. Somerset, NJ: John Wiley & Sons, 2011. Print.

Carducci, Bernardo J. *The Psychology of Personality: Viewpoints, Research, and Applications*. Somerset, NJ: John Wiley & Sons, 2009. Print.

Farah, Martha J. *Patient-based Approaches to Cognitive Neuroscience*. Cambridge, MA: The MIT Press, 2000. Print.

Gilman, Rich. *Handbook of Positive Psychology in Schools*. New York, NY: Routledge, 2009. Print.

Gonzalez-DeHass, Alyssa. *Theories in Educational Psychology: Concise Guide to Meaning and Practice*. New York, NY: Rowman & Littlefield Publishers, 2013. Print.

Martin, Carol Lynn. *Discovering Child Development*. New York, NY: Houghton Mifflin Company, 2009. Print.

McBride, Karyl. *Will I Ever be Good Enough?: Healing the Daughters of Narcissistic Mothers*. New York, NY: Simon & Schuster, 2008. Print.

Ray, Dee C. *A Therapist's Guide to Child Development: The Extraordinarily Normal Years*. New York, NY: Routledge Publishing, 2013. Print.

Santrock, J. W. *Life-Span Development*, New York, NY: McGraw-Hill. 2009. Print.

Shaffer, David R. *Social and Personality Development*. Belmont, CA: Wadsworth, 2008. Print.

Rick Wants to Help You and Your People!

Rick has spoken to many audiences around the United States bringing an energizing message of inspiration. He loves to help people find their hidden gifts and strengths, and shows them how to activate them.

Rick teaches people how to not only face their adversities and fears, but to allow difficulties to propel them further than they could go otherwise. He shows people how setbacks become stepping stones to something greater. Rick has countless true life examples of harsh adversities that were funneled and leveraged to help him grow. Your people will be inspired to do the same, and no longer be held back from living and working to their fullest potential.

Rick's primary keynote message, *"Secrets for Accomplishing the Impossible"* is a high energy and fast paced presentation that is guaranteed to energize and keep your people on the edge of their seats. This is a powerful motivational event that your people will talk about for months to come.

If you want your next special event to be truly spectacular, you'll want to invite Rick out to make your day more magical and exciting. You'll find Rick's Motivational Magic to be one of the most uniquely creative and inspiring programs available.

Rick impacts your audience with powerful visual effects, followed by content rich educational sessions, astounding true life inspiring stories and motivational messages. All carefully designed and crafted to create an atmosphere that helps your people break through the barriers holding them back from their greatest accomplishments.

The combined impact carries an intense emotional surge that creates the desire to step up and take action.

Why is this important? Rick says, "I have been to countless seminars and conferences over the years. Within 3 days, participants have forgotten 90% of what they were taught. By creating an emotional surge, what you are teaching becomes imprinted in their minds. The rate of retention and application now increases dramatically! Participants become committed to taking action that will have impact."

Your conference participants will say, "Rick was one of the best speakers we have ever had."

To hire Rick Saldan for your special event, visit his website at:

www.MotivationalMagic.com

9 781974 344901